AF290914

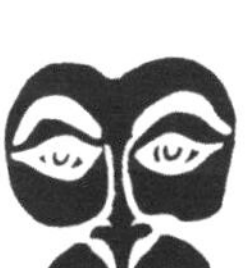

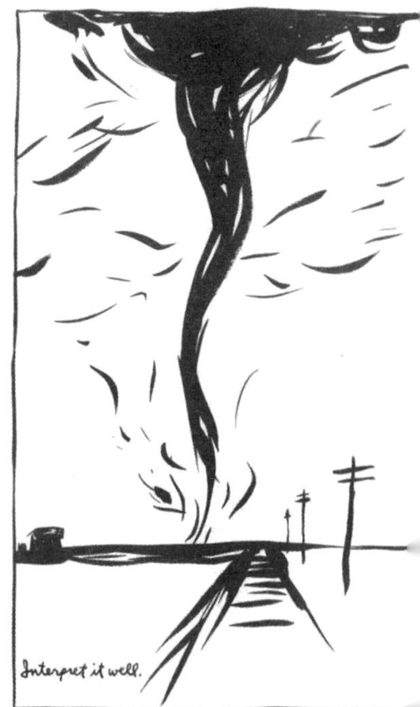
Interpret it well.

THE FRONTIER INDEX

Raymond Pettibon
& Mike Topp

ARTWORK BY RAYMOND PETTIBON

HANUMAN EDITIONS

1.

"Hey, what happened to everyone?"

"We don't know," said Dad,
standing on my head.

"We don't know," said Mom
in the cuckoo clock. "We don't
know. We don't know."

"I know," said my sister.

2.

Peas were bigger now, for one
thing. Much bigger. The size
of golf balls. And they weren't
green anymore. They were golf
ball-colored. And the pickles were
as big as watermelons. And they
didn't grow on trees anymore.
They grew in patches.

3.

Nothing surprises me now. I've
grown used to living in a world

*What a strange, demented feeling
it gives me when I realize I have
spent whole days before this ink-
stone, with nothing better to do,
jotting down at random whatever
nonsensical thoughts that have
entered my head.*

Kenko, Essays In Idleness, 1332

The Frontier Index

that is out of joint, as if it has been struck by an enormous earthquake so that the roads are no longer flat, nor the buildings straight.

Rolling a fatty loosey-goosey-like flat on my lap in my Fiat when Mama Mia the world turned off its axle: EARTHQUAKE! fortunately followed by a fire lit my joint.

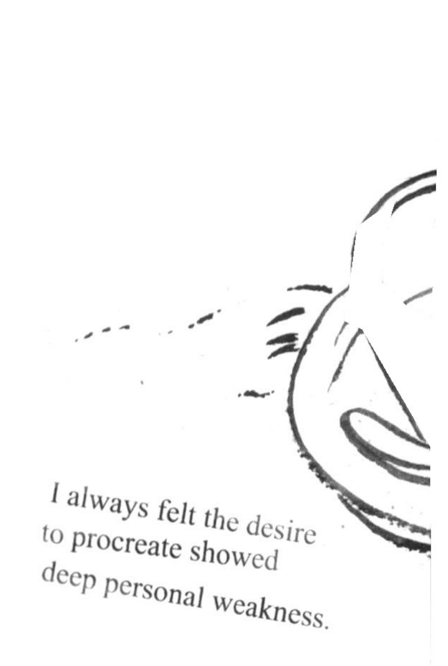

I always felt the desire
to procreate showed
deep personal weakness.

If there's one thing that really ticks me off, it's the meaninglessness of life.

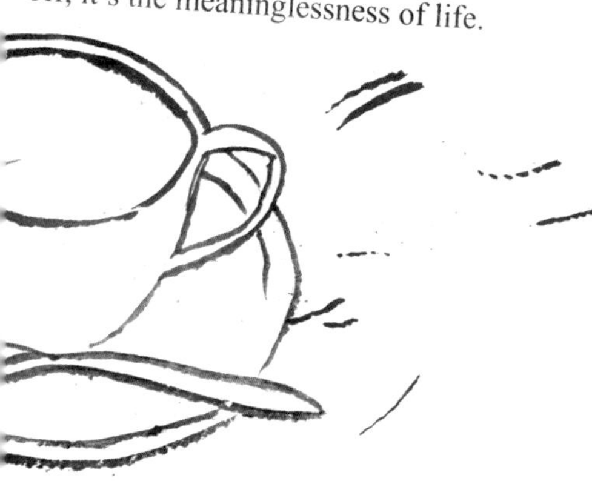

4.

At UCLA my professors (Alex
Trebek and then Hugh Downs)
explained it was hard to get
people to understand it's patriotic to be a traitor. It's a difficult
concept to understand because
it sounds so crazy when you first
hear it. Then you slowly start to
understand: Traitor = Patriot
Angela Davis spoke last Commencement.

On the whole I thought Angela
Davis's commencement speech

was pretty good. But maybe the "boinnnngggg!" sounds she put in after each couple of words hurt the tone.

5.

When Banzan was walking through the Union Square greenmarket he overheard a conversation between a vendor and his customer.

"Do you have chocolate mousse?" asked the customer.

"We have chocolate pudding," replied the vendor.

At these words Banzan became enlightened.

6.

Few books leave a deeper impression on readers young and old than Anton Chekhov's classic, "The Seagull." Interestingly, the play is an extensive reworking of Chekhov's original draft, which was entitled

"Jonathan Livingston Seagull."

7.

PATIENT: I dreamed I was doing somersaults across the Brooklyn Bridge (I'd bought the Brooklyn Bridge before it was even built) and my head blew out and I lost control.

PSYCHIATRIST: (interrupting) And you say this never happened?

PATIENT: No.

PSYCHIATRIST: (pause) I don't get it.

Triyp down perfect swan dive. Coming up I caught the bends. I remember occasionally asking passersby for a sandwich. I shldve gone to Steve Brodie's Bowery n Grand. Rated best "dive" Bar.

8.

As a jockey I had to occasionally take some shortcuts. Now when

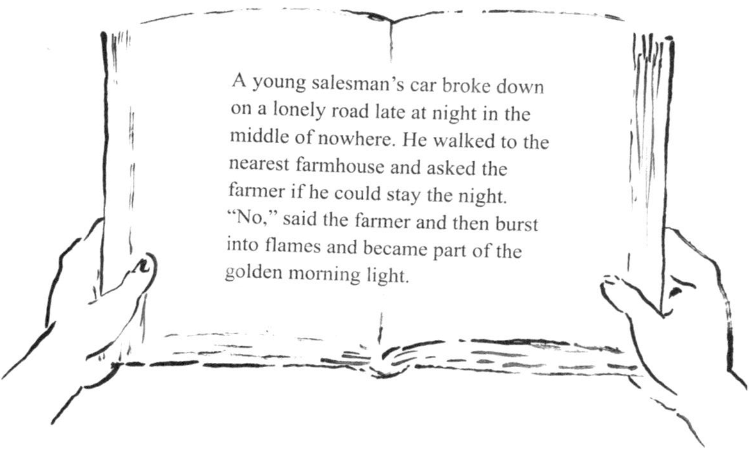

A young salesman's car broke down
on a lonely road late at night in the
middle of nowhere. He walked to the
nearest farmhouse and asked the
farmer if he could stay the night.
"No," said the farmer and then burst
into flames and became part of the
golden morning light.

my horse raced he was finished
practically before the others had
even gotten started, lazily swing-
ing back and forth in a hammock
on the finish line, sipping a Mint
Julep and wondering hey, what
kept you honest horses?

Many doubted Rosie Ruiz
could get the Marathon distance
but under my urging and strong
handling—don't spare the whip!
—she finished in record time.

Then I made everybody on
the street ride around on each

other like horses (where do I get my ideas?).

9.

MARLEY: Scrooooge! Ebenezer Scrooooooge!

SCROOGE: Who's that?

MARLEY: In life I was your partner, Bob Marley.

SCROOGE: What do you want?

MARLEY: To tell you you're doing a great job. Keep it up.

SCROOGE: Thanks, Marley.

SFX: DOOR SLAM.

10.

What started as a legitimate effort by the people of Salem City to root out those that used magic or supernatural powers to harm others quickly deteriorated into a witch hunt.

11.

Manhattan looked different.
There were no buildings at all.
People lived in caves, if they
could find them. Or on the
ground with a "cave view," if
that's all they could get. They
dressed in dried leaves and crud,
and ate the same stuff they were
wearing, sometimes while
wearing it.

12.

At first I didn't mind living next door to a mad scientist but after a while I started to get irritated by the insane laughter coming from his laboratory at all hours of the day and night.

13.

George Steele was the head writer at the start of the "Attitude Era," and the man most responsible for steering the company toward a newer "realism."

Soon the town was full of wrestlers, from the handsome movie star type of wrestler, kind of like me, to the goofy kind of wrestler with the laugh track instead of a theme song. Then there's George, destined to play Swedish wrestler and actor Tor Johnson in Tim Burton's film *Ed Wood.*

14.

Ma told me (I grew up in Yorba Linda): Anyone can grow up to be a Kennedy (President). But only one can grow up to be a Sirhan Sirhan.

Ma always told me I could be whatever I wanted to be when I grew up, "within reason." When I asked her what she meant by "within reason," she said, "You ask a lot of questions for a garbage man."

15.

SUSPENSE THEATER

MAN: After all we've been through together, do you think this is the end? Or could it perhaps be a new beginning?

WOMAN: I don't know. (PAUSE) I don't think we'll ever know.

(THE END)

16.

In the 1950s it was considered
unseemly if a well-bred young
woman married a carp, chub or
sucker. In those days, all three
were derided as "trash fish."

17.

Sometimes when reading
"Homer's Odyssey" on my
Kindle, things from other
genres—like an opera phan-
tom or a robot invader from

FOR ONCE LET ME BE AT PEACE, DON'T QUOTE ME.

FOR BAD UNSPEAKABLE THOUGHTS.

I hope everything you've said is in the public domain.

Last night I ordered a whole meal in Chinese. Even the waiter was amazed. I was in a French restaurant.

space—will suddenly pop up,
probably because I haven't
bought the ad-free version.
I thought I'd mention it. The
public has a right to know.
(U.S. Constitution, page 46)

18.

Ketamine is for kitty-kats, and
horse-pills for horsies. My doygs
eat sides of raw meat (horse and
cat). There is also a shrine in the
stable for Santo Malverde, if you

know what I mean.

The first trick Bad-Green Jesus tried to learn was how to turn his dogs into gold. The dogs thought he was kidding at first, and told him to cut it out, that tickles, but he told them to quit squirming and think gold. BGJ could retire if he could learn how to turn his dogs into gold.

Sacrificed many a doyg, chicken (we do cockfighting too), horse (horsemeat doesn't go to waste), and the occasional pig who wanders in not minding his business—all for the greater gooyd and higher payouyt.

19.

The phrase "Fortune favors the bold" originates in Virgil's "Aeneid," where it's uttered by an Italian warlord just before he gets killed.

20.

In the 1960s over half of the U.S. population was eaten by hippies.

Late '60's, '70s my Family lived in that bus, tumbled down Topanga Canyon Rd and we et well on pus, possums, and people.

The three P's!

21.

I explained to the court that when I was a kid my family had

had to sell my mouth to buy food, and later on, when the horse died and the new flat-screen TVs came out, the other mouth had to go. But it was all turning into too long a story, and was getting more unbelievable all the time.

A Horatio Alger Christmas Carol.

That lad went on to become Santa's little helper/supplier, head of the North Pole's production line with 150 elves working for him. Using his mouth to get ahead.

22.

Death continues to be our nation's number one killer. That was a Laff-In staple for one season only. Goyt tired, died.

23.

As a poeyt and professional wrestler some of my poetry was

published in the dirt sheets, but to the dismay of the major lit presses those pubs are hard to find! Working on newies till the original classics can be collected for reprints.

"The Iron Sheik's poems are often no more than a few lines, but when mixed with huge production budgets they dominate the ring." —Vince McMahon

24.

I wrote Strip (Sunset)? My bad (script grl c'mere trycck): (continuity) bytchs keep strippin as before (you tried out, now play out); Edith! Gimme Head! Edith: strip these bytchs from their 2-piece gowwwnnns. Thn ye dear. Now Miki Dora gets to strip th'bytchs tops, bottoyms, gowns. That Edith!

25.

"Twenty-five dollars. Payable in advance," I said.

"You'll get the money when you've finished mowing the lawn," said Mr. Wilson.

"Okay," I said, real tough.

26.

I think I paid too much for this certificate that says I'm an intellectual. Also the uniform. I goyt

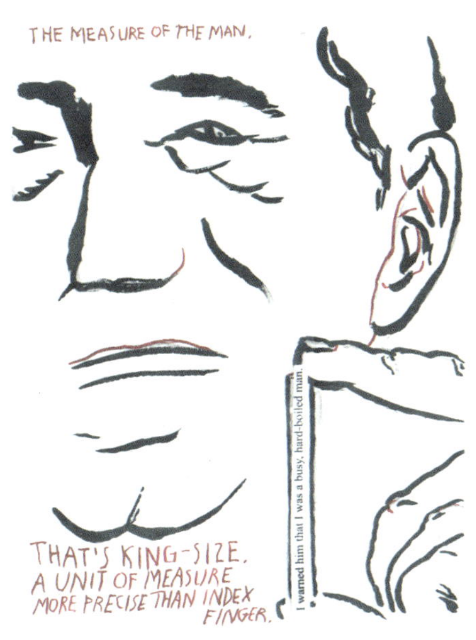

THE MEASURE OF THE MAN.
THAT'S KING-SIZE.
A UNIT OF MEASURE
MORE PRECISE THAN INDEX
FINGER.
I warned him that I was a busy, hard-boiled man.

mine from Oz Think Tank certi-
fying I'm a Public Intyllectual:
Continental Franco-German-
Israeli Savile tailored. A sporty
Bernard Henri-Levi Military cuyt
w/ribbons n croissants for pad-
ded elbows. Let me pose—well
I have been past 50 years.

27.

So, as if I didn't have enough
trouble of my own making
(those letter bombs come to

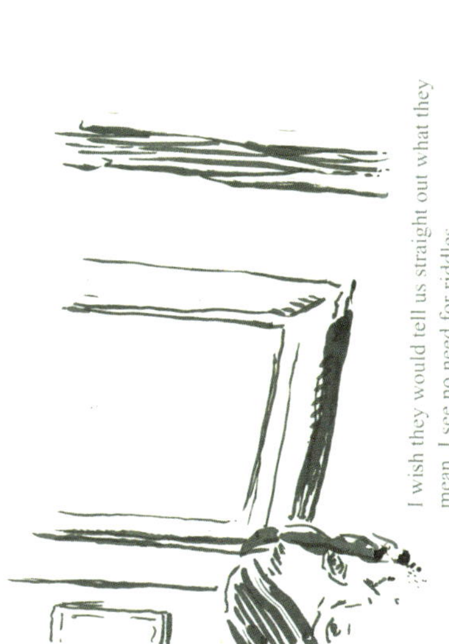

I wish they would tell us straight out what they mean. I see no need for riddles.

mind. And that threatening fruit basket I sent to the White House), now I had some crazy dame to deal with. Figures. The late Carl Werthman was right about when shit happens. It happens every time.

28.

I wondered where the Supreme Court justices got all those valuable paintings they had on the walls. And where some of the justices got those top hats they were wearing. "Wait," I said. "This is Whistler's Mother!"

"Used to be, maybe," said the chief justice. "It's my mother now."

29.

Flush for the week on my Belmont Stakes payday. Suggestions on how I should spend it? It's Monday, Wednesday's my parlay day.

30.

Drinking wine is a weekend thing with me, strictly Thursday to Tuesday. Tuesday is the best year.

31.

Before WWE, before OVW, Cena asked me to teach him how to wrestle and to rhyme. John was even greener in the ring than he was on the mic. Did I show him the ropes? Look at him now. He still can't wrestle, or rhyme—or act. Superstar.

Sounds like two warriors going at it with great respect for tradition. Did fingers find their way into places reserved for baser functions? You bet. But all of it happened in the fraternal spirit of male bonding, just like in olden times when men did stuff like that all the time.

32.

And just like you thought, it isn't your fault. It's everybody's fault but yours. So it's a happy ending for everybody.

Ain't my fckn fault. Campanis is the guy!

Not only that, the merchandising items produced by Campanis were seriously off-model. One of the Tommy Lasorda bobbleheads had Sandy Koufax's face and Roberto Clemente's backside. People said it

YOU CAN TEACH A DOG "KNOCK KNOCK" JOKES.

Burlap wrapped around your dog's face when he's hanging his head out of a car window will keep bugs from sticking in his teeth. From time to time it may be necessary to remove the burlap and clean it. However, a neater dog will result and grooming will not be so tiring.

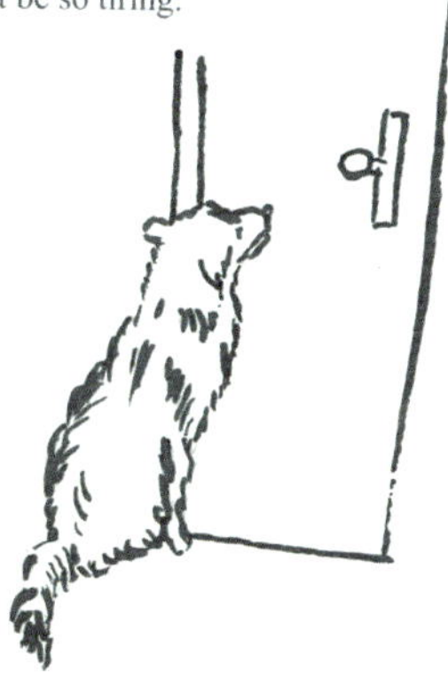

looked better than Lasorda usu-
ally looked, and maybe it did,
but that's beside the point.

Thought my Mr Coffee would
be a hit. Stopp'd working after a
week! And Koufax's bobblehead
wont work Sabbaths!

So running Campanis out
of town had, in the end, accom-
plished nothing. We had a broken
Mr Covfefe, but money isn't
everything. Koufax was often
AWOL, the reporters were still
annoying us with questions, and

the fans were still arriving in town in a never-ending stream.

Campanis left town gloating, thinking he'd made a strong point, and this last stunt rubbed it in: swimming from San Pedro to Catalina while towing Portuguese fishing boats and breaking Jack LaLanne's record.

33.

It's hard for Ken to have big dick energy.

My sisters' Ken-dolls were rather largish. From playing with 'em I guess. Or Play-Doh.

Ken worked occasionally as a crash test dummy, where he had just been blown apart for $5. He tipped me off about it while doctors were probing him for signs of life. My friend said he wouldn't be able to do any more work until somebody found the part of his head that said, "Okay."

Gay-Bob will have that.

34.

Mars Bar is always an amazing
and welcome sight to see when-
ever and wherever it magically
pops up—bright lights, peppy
music, good food and an amazing floor show with women
pulling rabbit ragu out of hats
and magicians sawing everybody's sandwiches in half. It's
a great place for a break. But
NIMBY. They wanted to give
it Historical Preservation status
to preserve th'fck ouyt of it.

Stonewall for drunks and junkies. Somehow that didn't take.

35.

Just finished reading Georges Bataille's amazingly prescient book "The Impossible Burger".

36.

Francis the Double-Talking Mule wasted lots of time getting into long philosophical discussions

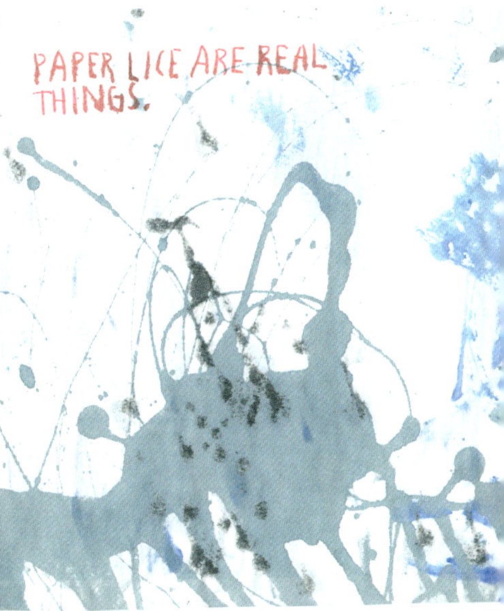

My mind is a raging torrent flooded
with rivulets of thought cascading
onto a waterfall of creative alternatives.

with the folks in the psych ward, saying things like "I'm not really a double-talking mule, you know. I'm a metaphor of mankind's carelessness and greed." Of course, everyone knew better.

37.

"Some of the Belmont Stakes horses went off-script. Noyt pleased." —Mr Ed.

38.

Gomer stuck his head in the door. "Barney said I should throw out the garbage," he said. "What's my motivation?"

"The garbage stole your girl," said Andy.

"It did? Why that dirty..."

Gomer left, thoroughly motivated.

39.

A monk asked Tozan when he was eating some pretzels: "What is Buddha?" Tozan said: "These pretzels are making me thirsty."

40.

I immediately dove into the exciting world of professional wrestling. I figured whatever I lacked in knowledge and experience I'd be able to make up for in enthusiasm and lack of knowledge. My crew included MI6, CIA, SMERSH and some old guy who changed clothes in a phone booth but was really scary.

41.

I wrestled 30–40 years territories to the respect of my peers, a [real] man's man, a worker's worker, and I was only elected (?a democracy?) to WWE as Lee Liberace's valet. And as a

songwriter working the Brill
and composing the songs of
yr life, elected RcknRoll HOF
for Mandy.

42.

I faced Wahoo but in the AFL in
the 60's playing Right Tackle for
KC Chiefs. Also used Indian gim-
mick, and he didn't like it, but
there was nothing he could do
abouyt it. Yes, I'm from Venice
but spent most of my time at

My new suit was incredibly wrinkly after I'd been shot, beaten, and left for dead. That's the trouble with linen.

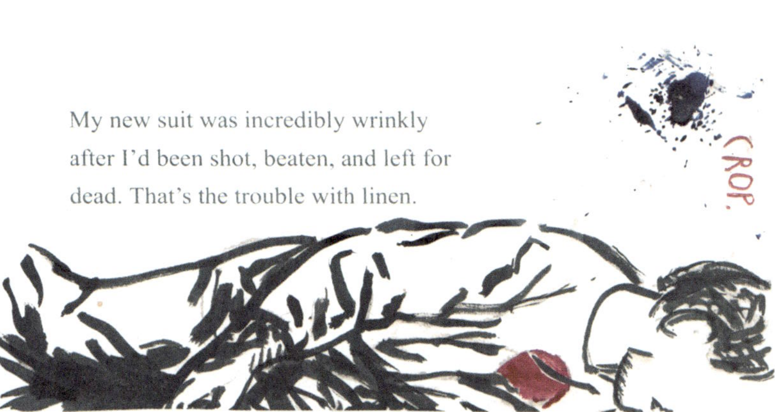

Gold's shooyting steroids n torturing bodybuilders.

43.

I got a new tuning fork. I've never seen meat vibrate this way before.

44.

I miss Lee Harvey Oswald.

45.

"Families is where our nation finds hope, where wings take dream," according to George W. Bush, our nation's 43rd president.

46.

It was hard to pay attention to the question Mom was asking because Dad was banging my head on the table to open some walnuts and some of them didn't want to open right away, and Mom was impatiently kicking my ass to make the answer come out of my mouth more quickly, which, well.

The question was this: q. Markedly sharper than the hammerhead and ma put the 'q' to me in her mouf asking: "I'll cuyt your balls; d'you understand me?"

47.

I told my associate he needed to act professional. He kept asking for advice about his personal problems—not having enough friends because he kept stabbing them, and how as he grew older, his hate was growing exponentially, is that normal? And sometimes his hate gets spots and so on.

48.

For a French semiotician from a
country not known for it (book-
ended by Carpentier and Andre
w/nothing between) Barthes
knew the business of pro wrestling, or to some, Sport Entertainment. Cld've made a great
booker. Sadly, in the end the
world, not ring, is the inhos-
pitable place!

49.

Two monks were arguing about whether their train was moving.

One said: "Our train is moving."

The other said: "The train on the tracks next to us is moving."

The Sixth Patriarch happened to be walking down the aisle. He asked them: "Would I look good in short shorts?"

50.

I won my first belt the hard way
behind the woodshed when instead of taking a serious beating
from my hillbilly pa I took the
razor strop and wrapped it
round my fist, cold cckd the
mfckr, my own kin n onetime
tag partner. I was 13.

51.

The next few days were kind of a
blur to Woody Woodpecker. He

didn't remember much of what happened. He kept a diary, but his entries for those days just said, "Guess who? Ha ha ha HA ha, ha ha ha HA ha, ha ha ha HA ha, hehehehehehehe!"

52.

We were looking for a good spot to try out my new bow-and-arrow set. It was getting dark. I tried for a bat overhead and missed but the arrow came

down and struck my brother.
Bats are really hard to hit the
way they dart and dive in the
sky. Dad said they're equipped
with a kind of radar.

53·

Wednesday, Friday, Monday, Sunday, Tuesday, Thursday, Saturday
—one week memorized in one
night (Monday or Tuesday, May
or June).

Dad was told by a fortune teller
he would die March 13, 2020.
The day came and went and
Dad, who had died eight months
previously, had the last laugh.

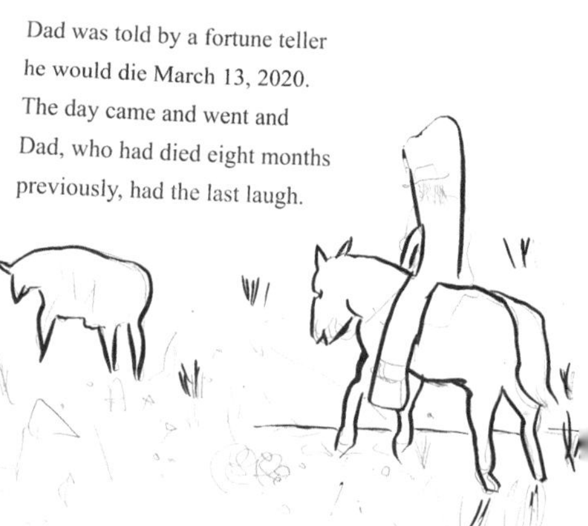

I do Wednesday to Sunday
because horseracing.

54.

We were pledging allegiance to
the flag and Dad caught me
looking out the window. Mom
said she didn't think that was
very patriotic of me. I said I was
looking at the flag outside on
the pole. Dad thought it over
and said from now on we were
to all look at the flag inside.

55.

When I came to, I was still in the headlock, only now King Charles was kneeing me in the face. I was starting to black out again. Why wasn't my family helping me? As I began to lose consciousness the awful truth finally hit me. He had bought them all off with his enormous wealth!

56.

I thought I was calling the match till I heard the ghosts of scripts past in the disembodied voice of Dick Lane. "Whoa nellie!" Every hold was returned w/force as me and the other became one tangled k8not of dynamic tension. There was no fixing this! No counts, no taps, but pop!

Rome wasn't built in a day, they tell me. Which I guess means we don't have to actually get anything done today, if we want to keep up with Rome. We've got an extra day to work with. We can take today off if we want.

57.

Mom said I could have anything I wanted for Christmas.

"Anything?" I asked, my eyes lighting up. (There was still a candle in my head left over from Halloween.)

58.

I was breaking into the Pro Wrestling game at same time as LA Knight. Soon found the money in the bank was in the Art hustle.

59.

I reminded them both not to make any false moves, and informed them that they were entitled to one phone call. "Good," said the taller of the two (Secretariat), pulling out his phone and starting to dial.

60.

Has anyone else noticed the expanding universe?

61.

The layoffs had begun. There were rumors that the company's name might be changed too, to Murder Incorporated. And the company logo—a clown slipping on a banana peel—was definitely out.

Restructuring, man. USMF-CKNGOVTUSSA logo. Siyt on th' flag.

62.

In my off hours I worked at performing biblical miracles. If Jesus can do it, I should be able to do it three times as well. Simple math. Change three glasses of water into wine instead of just the standard one. Or change them three times as fast. Three

times better, anyway, that's my
point.

63.

Early on, "Wheel of Fortune,"
the game show created in 1975,
had a segment in which players
are shown either being hauled
away to prison or lowered one by
one into unmarked graves.

64.

That's Dan, filmmaker trying to produce a life and Direct yours. We employ courtroom sketch artists for our storyboards. And that is the first, probly last. Action pic. Now roll the crediyts. Dan (with some help from Professor Exclamation Point) also came up with a first class mind control device. So now Dan is using the machine to force people to go to his picture, and to like it intensely no matter how bad it is.

65.

Mr Ed taught ME how to talk.
I was 2 n 1/2.

66.

"We need to inoculate ourselves
from the Kennedys, again and
again." —Sirhan Sirhan.

Some thought the CIA had
been involved in the Kennedy
assassinations. Few things could
be farther from the truth. Or

further from the truth, I wasn't sure which. Sirhan didn't know which one it was either. We decided it didn't matter.

Simple as fck, man. Trace it back to its source and: Sirhan, the original OG. Noyt Sirhan Sirhan. SIRHAN. Acknowledge Hiym.

67.

Lassie was finally canceled because of her big head. Sometimes

she wanted a rewrite, with a
better gag line here, and here.
Or she would keep calling in a
makeup artist to touch her up.
Or insisting on a stunt dog when
the abandoned mine Timmy had
fallen into looked too dangerous.

68.

I live in New York City and
consequently am never more
than six feet from either a rat or
being murdered.

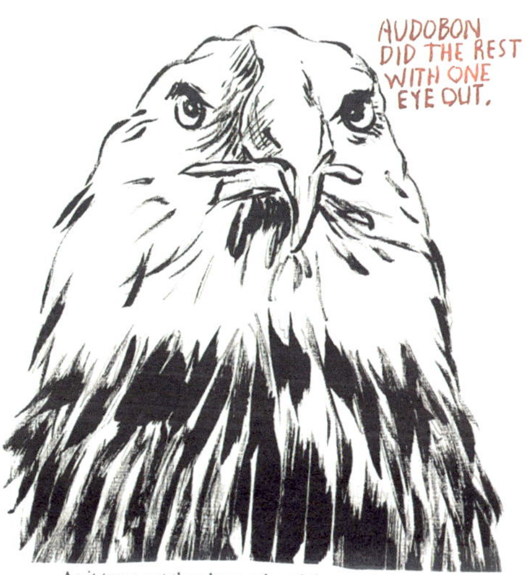

As it turns out they have relaxed the restrictions and I think your son should reapply. Make sure he wears protective clothing since he will most likely appear before one with a bird head, one with a rat head, and one with the head of a snake.

69.

Wife said I was impertinent,
hoping that doesn't mean what
I think it means.

70.

Was circling block looking for
Anne Bradstreet. You know, the
broad. Off Broad St? Noyt Ann
Streeyt?! Put up a parking lot
indeed. Poetry saves lives!

71.

Kayaking to Gibraltar, which is now almost completely under-water. She would soon land and summit on the Rock, as Noah did his arc on Mount Ararat during the floods. The kayaker lit his sinkproof pipe with a lighter that was wearing a small swimsuit. It fiyt well, tight as a drum, when I pull'd into Majorca.

"Majorca is covered with a thin water-resistant coating," the kayaker said proudly. "We can't hear the people anymore, but they're in there. And they won't sink."

Patch'd my speedos, tuck'd in. Buyt had to sac my right ball to make them fiyt. "This kayak can't sink because everything in it is unsinkable," the kayaker assured me. "Gee..." I said, pushing various nearby objects—including the kayak's cat and the kayaker's right ball—underwater, and then watching them pop back up.

Bobber n gunny sack. Both float.

72.

WTF. My iPhone was not up-dating. Several times I had attempted to fix it, this taking the form of turning it on and off. DIY skills exhausted, I settled into an easy chair by the wood stove.

Iyt saved my life once and now I can't turn it off.

My doctor told me to watch my iPhone usage, so now I use it in front of a mirror. It's got my best side.

Ah… Reflections…

Johnny Rangefinder.

Just what a gunfighter needs is a complex ethical problem. I thought about it, then told my conscience to take the rest of the day off, go watch a movie or something. If it bothered me again I'd blow its head off. That's the way you have to deal with things like that. A firm hand.

73.

Superstar Billy Graham died recently of steroid abuse 99 years old. The Living Legend got his start on Newsdance, the teen-oriented segment of the CBS Evening News, which featured the top headlines told to you by dance.

74.

When Mr Disney ("call me Wally") got in n checked me out I cld sense disappointment. Maybe because I was 17, too old for the Disneyland crowd. Though it didn't stop him from getting in the backseat w/me. I was only a gofer (for Nick Adams n Bob Conrad)—wht cld we possibly—CONT.

(CONT): talk about? Work? Nick n Bob worked, trawling Santa Monica for roles n role-plays. What did I have? Surprised indeed was I when my fly was unzipp'd and my cock hardened in Walt's mouth.

"What do you wish to be when you grow up? A movie star?" he asked. I told him the—CONT:

(CONT): truth. "A writer. A writer to the stars, w/someday my own gossip column." His gaze met mine, then wandered; I'd given him something to chew on. "No, tht wont do," he told me. "I wldnt hire you. Dnt know who wld." At that he coughed into his handkerchief and had the—CONT:

(CONT): driver drop me off,

on Hollywood. "Good luck with that one. Now I've heard every-thing." And he laughed. Before he could pull away I shouted at him: "My name's Bill! Billy Dakota." A name I made up on the spot, but one that would stick.

75.

That's how I look to sharks, man. Was a Great White; it took one I'm a ridgling now it's cooyl the shark left half its jaw thar—fck 'em they sck call me bless'd I produce sperm.

If you want to stay alive, then ante up. If you want to play it cheap, be on welfare the whole winter. I don't want no volunteers, I don't want no mates, there's just too many captains on this island. $10,000 for me by myself.

76.

Steven Seagal asked me if I could teach him the fine art of judo and submission holds. I respectfully (sic) declined and sent him to Gene Lebell. Gene also declined. And the only explanation Gene could think of to give Jonathan Livingston Seagal was a weak laugh—a laugh that got weaker the longer Gene looked at him.

77·

Inking and lettering Eisner panels was erasing myself.

"We live and learn, I've noticed." I got lost as requested and decided to get lunch. I asked the guy behind the counter if he had ever heard of anyone erasing themselves. "Every day, pal," he said. "You want to see life in all its permutations? Work behind a lunch counter." Erasing Wordsworth goyt me noticed.

As a poet, while I wanted to

be an editor.

Wordsworth called an eraser a "rubber," even when it was made of some petroleum-based substance. He also ate off paper plates that were really Styrofoam, wore glasses that were plastic, and used golf irons that were really titanium and woods that weren't. What are words worth? I blotted his ink.

I leaned up against a wall next to him and chewed a toothpick as he blotted Wordsworth's ink until I felt we had formed a loose bond. Then I said: "How's the blotting going?" I leaned up against a telephone pole like it was my own personal toothpick. "Chew tar!"

"Chew tar. Okay." I chewed on a telephone pole for a thoughtful moment. "I've got a ten-spot here needs a home."

"You interest me strangely. What are you asking for in exchange?"

"Information about an Eisner panel."

"Can you break a tenner with tarpennies?"

I winced. If he knew how much those Eisner panels cost he wouldn't tear them up like that. He wouldn't frame them or anything. They're not that valuable. But he wouldn't tear them up.

One sloww dissolvvvve.

78.

I couldn't believe I was meeting
Jerry Mander himself! He was
busily rearranging the country
with his hands, moving states
and cities around, considering
each new arrangement (big cities
first, most popular ones first,
alphabetical order, National
League and American League,
etc.).

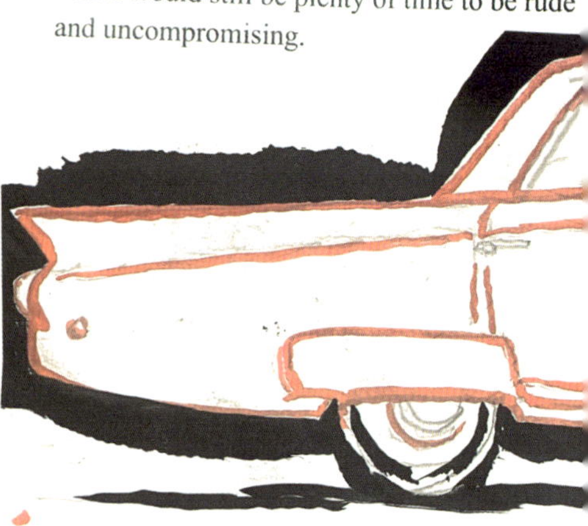

BY THE TIME YOU PAY FOR THAT
THEY'LL BE FLYING ROCKET SHIPS
TO WORK.

There would still be plenty of time to be rude
and uncompromising.

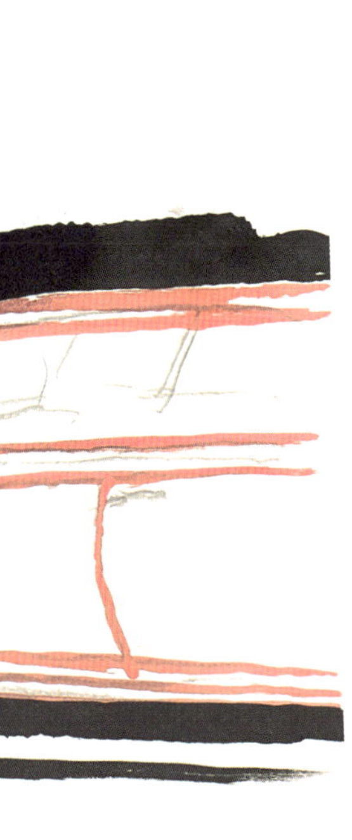

79.

There's a lot of snow here but it looked to me like my car might be able to make it, so I crossed my fingers, pushed the button that made the car hold its breath, and stomped on the gas.

"At least the heater's working."

As it turned out my car was just the right size to get halfway through the wormhole (at least the heater's working) but just a hair too big to get through the parts where they'd added all that snow. So I give myself credit for being half right. Score half a point for me.

Even Einstein couldn't figure this one. If it is to traverse space, a car must fit into its garage doors, but with its necessary tailfins. How?

As I tried to get my wedged-in car in the garage, I heard a lot of honking and looked in my mirror. My pursuers said the chase was over and the smart thing was to give up and be hauled away for a fair trial and a speedy execution. That's what the smart set was doing this year, they said.

Wait till the next model hi-test, self-flying Teslas come ouyt, Elon will thrust you into space in your erector seat save on gas, Tang, astronauts.

"Tang!" we all said at once, with some of us saying it over bullhorns.

There was a terrible malfunc-tion while pissing involving Grissom and his roasted freeze-dried bull nuyts. A can of NASA-developed Fresca with cyclamates enriched Retsyn put ouyt the electrical fire and saved further lives from an unpleasant funerary death.

Gruff Gus Grissom was left stranded and alone in the middle of nowhere with his pants down. And if that wasn't the story of his life before, it was now.

80.

I'm so hungover I've completely forgotten how to blow my own nose. Still can't remember. How do you do that? You push the handkerchief up your nose, and then what?

Snow packed you will need a snow plough.

81.

From the manger gift shop I'd purchased a bold new swimsuit and caftan that were definitely working. I was getting more than my share of looks! (That swimsuit was hands-down my favorite for years until my associate Don Knotts told me it was a pair of women's underwear. Carpe diem!)

82.

Hippie Jesuys at Venice Beach.
Trying to dismiss Him as a sort
of inspired fairy. Buyt He can
surf. Hard to diss that. Goofy
fooyt. And feeyds the people.

83.

"Locals only, punk," He said.
I sidestepped His attack and
gave Him a karate chop. Something like Thor's hammer came
down on my head and I started

to wobble. I dove at Him and grabbed on for dear life. It slowly dawned on me that Jesus was enjoying the close contact with another man.

84.

I've bleached my long, flowing locks for some time now (Ma wanted a Shirley Temple). Goyt a gripe? All the stars do iyt: Marilyn, Mansfield, Harlow, Dors. The Babydolls n faces. AND ALL

the PRO WRESTLERS YOU LOVE
(and some you love to hate).

85.

I'm gonna admit it: When Sister
Bertrille showered with us after
wrestling practice there were
more than a few boners on dis-
play. It wasn't very respectful,
but it was hard not to think of
her as just an ordinary woman
even though she'd given over her
life to serve only Jesus Christ.

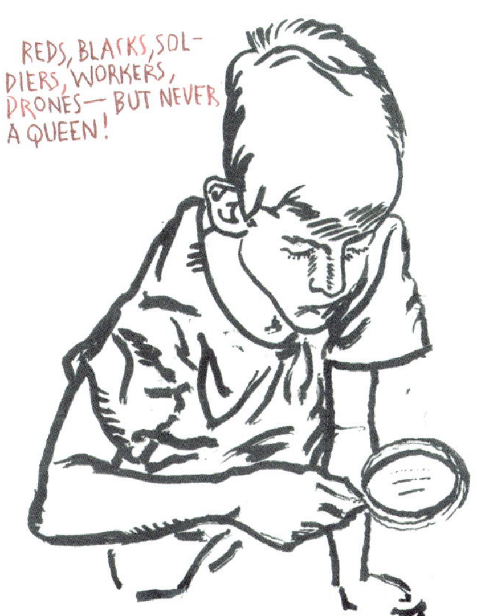

That same woman who told me this was the quiet car just got up and told another guy the same thing.

86.

Did you meet ever Bob Barker? I'm still kinduva fanboy for Bob, who's no fan of WWF because they tried to recruit Vanna and he's like me a PETA fan, dosent give a fck abouyt wildlife. We're naming a wing (sic) of our Canine Sports Entertainment complex for Barker.

Also, surprised that Vanna didn't go over to the WWF— because she was a joiner in high school. Pillow Fluffers Club,

Glum Club, Pillow Queen Society, Pyromaniacs Society, Friends of Foucault, Society of Blimp Repairmen, Whig Party, Vince McMahon Study Group—she did just about everything.

87.

This year's Scrabble tourney had the usual ice sculptures of Kama Sutra scenes and live exotic animals on chains. Although I wasn't the biggest celebrity at the gathering (Carrot Top and Kathy Griffin were both in attendance) I felt right at home surrounded by all this style and class.

88.

As director Chad Stahelski and I drove around Hollywood together, I took the opportunity to talk shop with him. I asked him things like: When John Wick throws his gun at somebody, how does he get it back? Because he's only got one gun. And he just threw it away. Now what happens?

In rapt attention at cinema, I look for one flaw, one anomaly, which spoils the picture for me even as it gained me internet fame n fortune as the guy behind "What's Wrong With This Picture?" But now I see that these "flaws" had directorial intent. Opie put em in.

Opie to Aunt Bee: "So sweet

the kiss, so smooth the shoulders, the sound of your clothes rustling over your Aunt Bee boulders."

BTW Opie's rap game goyt him nowhere with B.

89.

Those were different times.

"How's it going, son of a whore?"

"When was the last time you took a bath?"

Totally predictable small-town-type stuff. A bygone era really. Apple pie. Napalmed fishing villages.

Opie caught that big-ass carp with cherry bombs and blasting caps. Now it's a cement pond. Kilt all the catfish too. Was necessary to destroy th'ol' swimming hole in order to save it. Opie! C'mere n show Bee how big!

Opie and Aunt Bee would occasionally meet in a small clearing in the woods that was unknown

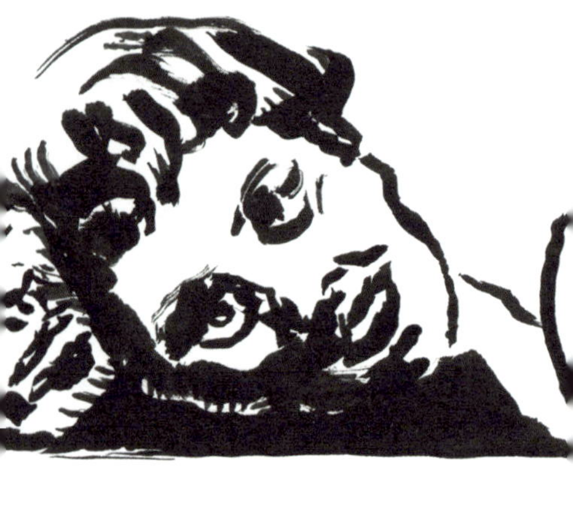
THE BOWELS OF
MUSEUM.

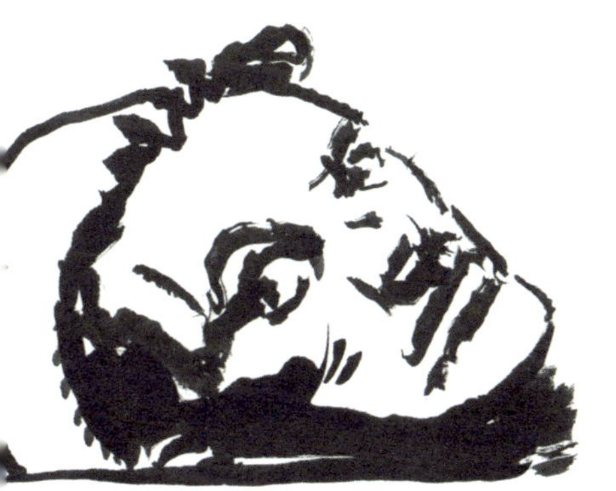

THE BRITISH

"Nice bowels," I said.

but to them. Opie later had "The Love Letters of Opie Taylor and Aunt Bee" privately printed, with the disclaimer that these were the simple yearnings of a 12-year-old boy addressing a love 52 years his senior (May December).

It's whispered that young Truman the Capote boy ghostwrit those same letters to enflame the local matrons for not entirely embracing his company, and bring most welcome and deserved scandal upon his own person.

I also heard Truman Capote once took noted tennis legend and feminist Billie Jean King to the cement pond with the intention of throwing her in. He was steaming mad at her—but he wasn't a murderer. As for his later alleged affair with Nelda Linsk: Answered Prayers (Rimshot).

That would be a surprise to Billie Jean and a shock (and con-firmation) to the gossiyps at the racquet club. Truman, high-strung as cat gut, was well-known to play around, but only pickle or paddle, and never mix or misce doubles with the likes of Dinah Shore or Ruta Lenska.

90.

My money's on Tajiri or Sei Shōnagon. But what we need around here now is somebody with common sense. Right now all we've got are people who know what they're doing. But

nobody listens to me. Nobody
ever listens to me.

91.

No signings in airports. I have
standards and so should you.
(But if I'm sleeping one off go
ahead and ring me up at the
hotel gotta make that plane).

92.

Just on the off chance that my wrestling career might be interesting to others I wrote up my life story and sent it to Hollywood, but they said it sounded like a bunch of movies they'd already made. They said I owed them money. I checked with a lawyer. She said I'd better pay them.

I officially announced my retirement from wrestling to the press the next day. I said I wanted to spend more time with my family. No one was interested, and I think a lot of them knew I didn't have a family.

I am the only ex-Pro Wrestler who did a shooyt podcast interview and did not say a word for 3 hours.... I won't break kayfabe, I won't expose the business, I won't incriminate my opponent or tag team partner, face or heel. There should be more like me.

93.

Some kayfabe got mixed up with my groceries somehow—most notably the limburger cheese (in the kitchen?)—so now I was super strong but I smelled super strong too. So I was still kind of a great Pro Wrestler ("Help us StinkMan!" "Here I am!" "Eww!"), but what kind? See what I mean?

94.

If I turn'd babyface—which I am
—then I would lose my many
Followers. NOYT GONNA HAP-
PEN!!!

95.

Sheikh Mohammed bin Rashid
al Maktoum supports new down-
town racetrack replacing Belmont
and Aqueduct, says clearing
ground ready to commence
anytime. In the meantime, the

horses will run their races up
and down the escalators at
Macy's Herald Square.

96.

At the French Dinerette in the
Old Country they offered escar-
gots or cheval? I had to ask.
Snails or horse. Gimme both
m'sieur. The "cheval" (fancy for
horse) could've been one of my
own plodders I'd sent over if
it wasn't tough n gamey. Mine

never were. Ran like snails.

"It's almost time for our regular Sunday cheval chowdown! Join us. You'll enjoy it. Good food, good laughs, and we've kidnapped the police chief to dance for us." (Coming Soon: Lost Snails Day or Where Did Escargot?)

97.

Don't blame horse, blame jockey. I tell myself. But then there's the trainer, and they're only in it for themselves. If I could drop that last jockey into a $3500 claimer for jockeys and sell off that lil' mfckr I surely would. But you can't do that nowadays. So I take the loss.

By the way, I'm half-man, half-horse (I'm a horse on the inside). I'm a jockey too (documents on file).

98.

I handed him another baseball card. "On this Jim Fregosi," I said, "I want you to write a poem about me. Compare me to a beautiful flamingo, flying across in front of a sunset. Remember to compare me favorably, don't make it sound like the flamingo is better than me. Then sign your name."

99.

"This card has my birth date wrong," he said, pointing at the stats on the back. "And my lifetime batting average is .327, not .237." He looked at the front again. "And this picture on the front isn't me. It's Marv Throneberry."

"Just sign it," I said.

"Oh, all right."

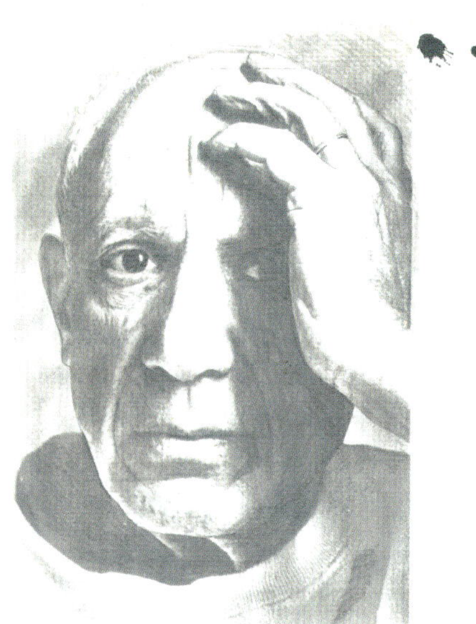

PICASSO'S PENCILS.

"How many monkeys even own typewriters anymore?"

100.

D.B. Cooper landed on me. I told him he was supposed to land in Vancouver, not on top of me, and I expected him to replace my hat with one just as good. He wandered off, dragging his parachute behind him, looking back at me like I was a jerk or something. The feeling's mutual, pal.

Landed on me buyt noyt dead center I felt unloved unwanted why? there noyt here non+'d no bullseye u sck take me home this is on you this is war buy me silk stockings@5%&()*+(&)_()

101.

Art Instruction Inc. was a fully accredited asterisk art school that could teach me everything footnote to start me on my guaranteed road to a successful see disclaimer career in art asterisk footnote mousetype. And all it would cost me was $795.

The matchbook couldn't believe
it.

102.

My 12.5 Claimer died doing
what iyt loved: losing; and was
"humanely destroyed" out of
sight n out of running. I asked if
it could be buried in walking ring
with the Forego's, War Admirals,
Sea Biscuits. They offered their
own choice: infield or parking lot,
bring my own shovel.

They finally decided he could be buried with Mr. Ed (parking lot). Oh, and for some reason they also asked me to draw a pirate.

"Of course," I said. I know how the world works.

103.

At no point, now or ever, did I aspire to make art to line the walls of creepy lawyers or the galleries that cater to them.

104.

Mr Nudie sewed something
extra into the sole of my cuban
heel booyts, if you know what I
mean. A certain foreign object,
call iyt, packed w/the payload
of Cuban missiles, but made by
Nudie in the gooyd ol' USSA.
Why I had a limp? Check ouyt
that jobber's jaw.

It's the naysayers who get me.
I think everyone in the world
took it for granted that I wouldn't
have the balls to wear Mr Nudie

Cuban heels even though forbidden by Dad. I've got the balls, big hairy misshapen balls in a wrinkly sack. This book is a testament to my giant balls.

You told me you're a ball nuts model (nickname Bull Nuyts), not a fooytsie booytsie model. What gives? Impossible to be best in the world at both.

105.

If you ever jump out of a plane, and your parachute doesn't open, don't worry. Worry won't get you anywhere.

LSD does that to me. And DMT—short triyp, man.

If there's long Covid, there's definitely long trips from LSD —no joke, I've dropped acid Friday night and then had some more blotter Saturday night. I still have flashbacks about when JFK told me he used to enjoy

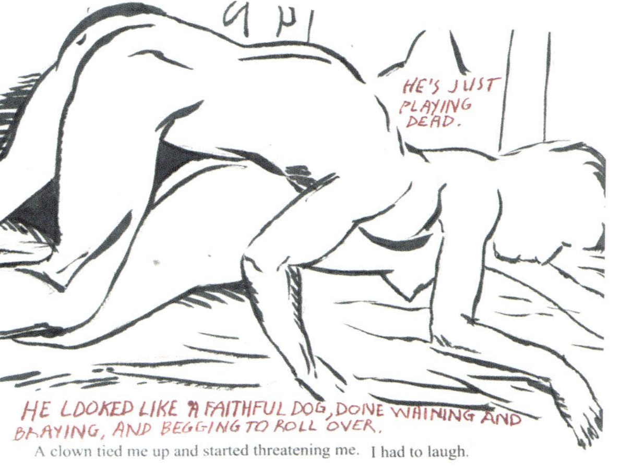
HE'S JUST PLAYING DEAD.
HE LOOKED LIKE A FAITHFUL DOG, DONE WHINING AND BRAYING, AND BEGGING TO ROLL OVER.
A clown tied me up and started threatening me. I had to laugh.

Marilyn Monroe from behind while Joe DiMaggio looked on in the corner.

Marilyn and Jack shared many a long triyp on LSD, mescaline, STP—buyt Marilyn took the short triyp home. Downs.

The main players have all left the stage, so perhaps now is the time to speak out without fear of reprisal: "She was a victim of soicumstance."

106.

First baseman "Dirty Jack" Doyle (Ireland) brought an artistic eye to MLB and a kind of European nihilism that was completely unnecessary. Oftentimes our disagreements were trivial, like the time we argued over which dog breed, Weimaraner or collie, was better at learning tricks.

First to break the color barrier against Black Irish ballplayers.

Dirty Jack carried on a feud with John McGraw that started

when they were teammates at Baltimore. McGraw, of course, had to have the last word. In 1902 McGraw was named manager of the Giants, and he released Doyle, even though he was batting .301 & fielding .991. Suck it, McGraw.

Neither Doyle or McGraw were ones to be fckd with.

107.

Always put a loyt of miles on my Cadillacs. But working the southern territories, ran the moonshine too—supplemented my income but gooyd.

I should've looked at a map but in those days they didn't have maps so I headed for Georgia anyway. Days later I was in Alabama and getting kind of frustrated. I sometimes wonder how the other moonshiners even do it. How do they get from one place to the next without getting lost? The stars?

I'm doing 500 on the I-70 Speedway doyg. Hard to get lost on the oval.

When I got to Indianapolis I hadn't slept in three weeks and hadn't shaved or showered. My clothes smelled like farts and clams and were stiff from roadside sweat and dirt. Big problem: My moonshine delivery was due in 5 minutes! My first time in the Indy 500... and I knocked it out of the park.

NASCAR'rrs load their trunks full of moonshine for ballast.

108.

If you remember Captain Kangaroo, he always claimed he wasn't a real captain. In fact, he was the original captain of the SS Minnow. One time a reef tore up the hull good. Only the Captain and I survived the sinking. In the lifeboat he tried to eat me but I grew to like him anyway.

Canceled and ran out his retirement pushing barges on the East River as tugboat Captain. Hated it when kids asked him to pull iyt and blow iyt. As mythical as Sully to some, but to the kids all too real. Liked him in B&W too—was always white to me.

I worked in the boiler room in return for passage home to Manhattan. How I got to Brooklyn is another story. We spent nights drinking rum until we passed out. The Captain—his real name was Bob Kooky-Jello but he went by Ogg in those days—left the tugboat's navigation to Mr Moose.

Whoever was at the wheel that drunk zig-zagging was too much for Sully's 747. While I swum from Ellis awash n shook it off, glad to have missed (by a lash) Bob's welcoming advances.

Mr Moose was a great navigator but was unfamiliar with New York Harbor and got confused. When Bob woke up he thought we were off Ellis when in fact we were off the coast of Peru. Those are some of the toughest waters to navigate for moose or man and, well, Mr Moose wasn't up to it.

Moose was up to his nose in snow and digging it like his natural habitat.

109.

While I was debating whether to go back to the bank and try it again, maybe this time claiming I had a gun, or claiming that I'd had a gun the last time, but didn't now, I suddenly remembered the many explanations I'd received from Willie Sutton about how that's where the money is.

"Don't you know who I am?" Apparently they didn't and I had to pull ouyt the heavy artillery: "I know Willie Sutton." That drew their attention, and the tellers, even the Bank President swarmed 'round to hear stories

while some creepazoid pull'd
the silent alarm.

Willie Sutton and I ran a cock-fighting ring for years. (I was still a "beginner" crook.) We ran 20 fights every Friday night. He bred his own gamecocks, cut off the comb and wattle himself to prepare them for the fights and raked in a small fortune. He named his best cock "Sir Willie."

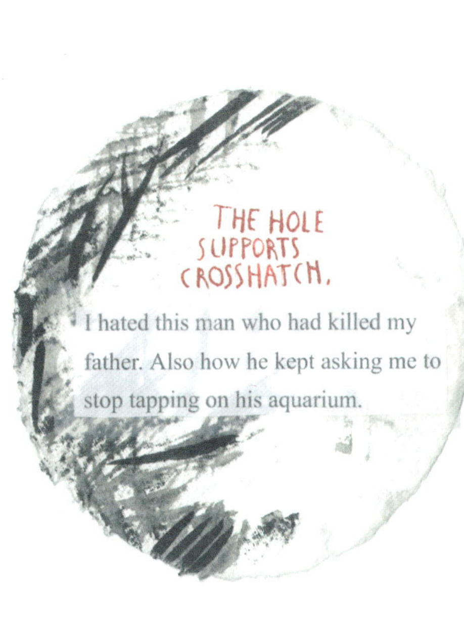

I hated this man who had killed my father. Also how he kept asking me to stop tapping on his aquarium.

110.

I explained to Bugs Bunny
that using the portable-hole
invention was a misdemeanor,
whether Elmer Fudd fell in it or
not, and he was trying to talk
his way out of a ticket by saying
Wile E. Coyote was always paint-
ing train tunnels on canyon walls.
I said it was a false equivalency.

111.

Sometimes my coworkers' suspicions would be aroused by items they found in my pockets when they were stealing from me—my search history, my algorithms, that sort of thing—or by things I shouted in my sleep when I was sleeping on the job, like "You'll never take me alive, pigs!"

112.

"A smart refrigerator isn't just a novelty item, you know," the salesperson said.

"What else is it?"

"It's an indispensable part of any smart home."

"Ah."

"Think about it."

"I will."

"Talk it over with your smart toilet."

"Okay."

113.

Two years ago, seismologists at UCLA predicted an earthquake in Haiti. Sadly, they were right. A magnitude 7.2 earthquake struck Haiti on Aug. 14, 2021, causing widespread destruction. The good news is that two of the seismologists will receive the prestigious Bruce Bolt Medal.

114.

"Hello?" I said. There was no reply. I heard sinister music on the line. "Is this Murder Incorporated?"

115.

Our family didn't have anything to do one afternoon so we all made cookies. I thought Dad's were the best but Mom thought mine were. Dad voted for Mom's and so did my sister, so Mom

won. Mom admitted afterward
that she thought hers was the
best but didn't think it right to
vote for herself. Dad thought
mine would have won if I had
kept them simpler. Everyone
criticized my sister's on tech-
nical grounds.

116.

In the beguine was the Word,
bytch. Period. This isn't Insta-
gram doyg: no illuminators,

illustrators, letterers, inkers,
no colorful ribbons no purple
prose. For yr illumination.

The Word is both divine and
eternal in nature, as I was recently reminded by my editor George
Steele, who as always has been
ever watchful and patient, reading over many drafts of my most
recent manuscript as well as
cleaning my gutters.

(He sounds like a great guy.
You must deserve such treat-
ment.)

Why there are many treatments.

George's supermarket shopping cart is always weighted down with cuts of red meat... and NO CHICKEN.

Of course. Editors are expert butchers. They know their marbling.

117.

Can you print this uyp no?
Homie I neeyd a mode of
engagement puyt this on
paper or....

ABOYT THE AUTHORS

Raymond Pettibon is an American artist who lives and works in New York City. Pettibon came to prominence in the early 1980s southern California punk rock scene; over the past three decades, he has become widely renowned for his iconoclastic—read, "fuck off"—use of motifs pulled from the high (literature, art history, philosophy, religion) and low (politics, sports, sexuality) to engage in "a steady indictment of American culture as he has lived it over the past 60 years."

Mike Topp was born in Washington, D.C. and currently lives in New York City unless he has died or moved. An emissary of enigma long before the era of the anon, Topp's work moves between poetry, art criticism, satire and sloganeering in whimsical koans with an indelibly deadpan élan. Recent collaborative books include *The Double Dream of Spring: A Peg Sluice Mystery* with Sparrow, and *Born On A Train* with Raymond Pettibon.

The Frontier Index
Raymond Pettibon & Mike Topp

Published by
Hanuman Editions
London & Seattle
hanumaneditions.com

Founding Editor: Shruti Belliappa
Co-Editor: Joshua Rothes
Editorial Assistant: Moselle Kleiner

Publishers: Shruti Belliappa, Joshua Rothes
Design: Shruti Belliappa, Joshua Rothes
Typesetting: Joshua Rothes

Hanuman Editions is designed, edited, and published by Shruti Belliappa and Joshua Rothes, in friendship.